Writing Funny Bone Poems

by Paul B. Janeczko

SCHOLASTIC
PROFESSIONAL BOOKS

NEW YORK · TORONTO · LONDON · AUCKLAND · SYDNEY
MEXICO CITY · NEW DELHI · HONG KONG

DEDICATION

For Pat Lewis
funny guy and good friend
good guy and funny friend

Riddle poems on page 6 by J. Patrick Lewis. Copyright © 2001 by J. Patrick Lewis. Used by permission of the author.

"The Cow," "The Mule," "The Fly," "The Porpoise," "The Ostrich," "The Termite," by Ogden Nash.
Copyright © 1931, 1953, 1942, 1942, 1957, 1942 by Ogden Nash. Reprinted by permission of Curtis Brown, Ltd.

Brat poems on page 18 by X. J. Kennedy. Copyright © 2001 by X. J. Kennedy. Used by permission of the author.

Senryu on page 22 by Kristine O'Connell George. Copyright © 2001 by Kristine O'Connell George.
Used by permission of the author who controls all rights.

Limericks on page 31 by April Halprin Wayland. Copyright © 2001 by April Halprin Wayland. Used by permission of the author.

From *I Spy School Days: A Book Of Picture Riddles* by Jean Marzollo, photographs by Walter Wick.
Published by Cartwheel Books, a division of Scholastic Inc. Text copyright © 1995 by Jean Marzollo.
Reprinted by permission. *I Spy* is a registered trademark of Scholastic Inc.

Cover design by Jim Sarfati
Cover poem adapted from a poem by X. J. Kennedy.
Interior design by Solutions by Design, Inc.
Cover illustration by Tamara Petrosino
Interior illustrations by Mike Moran

ISBN: 0-439-07349-9

TABLE OF CONTENTS

Introduction

Most of us enjoy a good laugh. We love sitcoms, stand-up comics, and the cartoon pages of the newspaper. Many medical experts assure us that laughter can be powerful medicine. Laughter can also be an important part of our classrooms. It can defuse a tense situation, it can help everyone relax, and it can keep our attention on the sunny side of things. Humor can also give students a chance to shine in their writing.

Make no mistake about it. This book is *not* about writing gags for a stand-up comedian. It *is* a book about writing many kinds of humorous poetry. Some forms, like the limerick and the riddle, are classics. I hope others are new to you. You will read humorous poems by some of the top poets writing for kids, like J. Patrick Lewis and Kristine O'Connell George.

When I say "humorous" poetry, I don't mean you and your students will be writing fall-down-laughing jokes, but much of it will crack up everyone who hears it. Most of the time the poems will be quietly clever—they will rely on magical wordplay for effect. By writing the poems in this book, your students will learn the delight of fooling around with language—with *their* language.

Writing humorous poetry gives students a chance to experience their world in a slightly different way than they are accustomed to experiencing it. More than that, it gives them a chance to share their vision with other students and with adults. Poet Jonathan Holden writes that the purpose of poetry is "to give shape, in a concise and memorable way, to what our lives feel like." Further, he notes that poems "help us notice the world more and better, and they enable us to share with others." We all know that few exchanges can match the joy of sharing a laugh or a smile!

Because some of these forms of poetry might be new to you and to your students, each lesson begins with a Poetry Page that presents examples of the poetic form of the lesson. This is followed by a brief introduction to the form, its origins, and its characteristics.

Next, in each "Exploring the Poem" section, I highlight essential aspects of the particular poetic form. I might explain the type of content the poem requires or the structure of the form itself. Occasionally, I suggest some questions that you might ask to help you begin exploring the form with your class. I usually offer an activity that might help your students understand and become familiar with the characteristics of the type of poetry.

The "Brainstorming" and "Drafting" sections are designed to help you get your students past writer's block, the common fear of having nothing to write about. Brainstorming and drafting allow students the chance to try out some of their ideas without the pressure of feeling that their poem must be perfect as soon as they put pencil to paper.

Each poetry activity is followed by a section called "Extending the Lesson." In it I suggest some ways in which the poetry-writing lesson can be expanded, perhaps into a performance, a display, or a connection to another curriculum area. I've no doubt that you'll see other ways to extend the lesson so your kids can see that poetry can be found in every aspect of our school days and every aspect of our lives. Finally, I suggest some books that include more examples of the poems used in the lesson.

You need not start at the beginning of the book and work your way through to the last page. Pick and choose what works best for your kids at each particular time of the year, in a way that complements work you are doing in other curriculum areas. It is wise, I think, to mix these humorous poetic forms with other, more serious poetry-writing activities. (See my *Favorite Poetry Lessons* and *Teaching 10 Fabulous Forms of Poetry* for ideas.) However, when you take this book from the shelf, no matter which activity you are using, remember one thing: Have fun!

Riddle Poems

by J. Patrick Lewis

The sky shook,
The wind tossed
Me in the air.
Toto-ly lost,

I came upon
Three strangers. We
Kept each other
Company.

Adventures followed
Without pause,
And it was all, well
Just bec-Oz.

[about Dorothy in *The Wizard of Oz*]

What starts
with D,
ends with D,
has a D
in the middle,
and makes
you turn
your car
around?   [about a dead end]

The
mystery
inside this
breakfast snack
is not a very hard
case to crack. It's
just a roundabout
excuse for mak-
ing other hens
and roost-
ers.

[about an egg]

Riddle Poems
And Therein Lies the Challenge

A riddle is an indirect description of a person, place, thing, or idea. It is written, of course, in a way that will puzzle the reader. As a poetic form, riddles have been around for hundreds of years in the literature of many cultures. An important English collection of riddles dates from the tenth century! Of course, kids have probably come up with riddles on their own for even longer than that. You can probably remember some of the riddles from your childhood, such as, "What's black and white and red [read] all over?" Poetic riddles build on that tradition of humor and cleverness by adding rhythm and sometimes rhyme.

The riddle poems on the Poetry Page at the beginning of the unit were written by J. Patrick Lewis, who has written many highly regarded poetry books for young readers, including two tantalizing collections of riddles. He offers this advice to would-be riddle-writers:

> The success of a riddling depends upon the answer *not* being too obvious. If it's too easy, readers will think it's simply dumb; if it's too hard, they will think it's impossible. So striking the right balance between dumb and impossible is what you want to do.

And therein lies the challenge.

EXPLORING THE POEM

The Key Is in Each Word

Like any good poem, a successful riddle relies on careful word choice. Finding exactly the right word is rarely easy. As Lewis says, "Your first effort shouldn't be your last." Word choice is especially crucial for a riddle because the poem must be puzzling fun—both a clever description *and* a challenge to the reader.

Let your students read Lewis's riddles, and note that in a good riddle, words often have two meanings. In the poem about Dorothy and Toto, for example, Lewis uses two phonetic double meanings: "Toto-ly" and "bec-Oz." Students who are familiar with *The Wizard of Oz* will immediately get the puns. In the egg riddle, Lewis writes that it is "not a very hard / case to crack," which is a wonderful play on words. In this instance the whole phrase, not just an individual word, holds two meanings. In riddle poems the second meanings are clues to the solution to the riddle. This type of double-meaning wordplay is a fun challenge for the reader to puzzle out. It is also a fun challenge for the poet to create!

BRAINSTORMING

Spinning a Web

Your students can begin drafting their poems by picking a subject. They can write down a number of ideas in their notebooks until they find one that strikes their fancy, be it a person, place, thing, or idea. Everyday objects make great subjects. I suggest keeping it simple, but it could be something from science, sports, school, the body, or even outer space.

Once students have chosen a subject, they can make a web or diagram, with that subject in the center (see sample at left). They can then write down characteristics of the object, from the most obvious to the most extraordinary. They should arrange the characteristics in circles connected to the center of that web. Creating this diagram will help students keep track of and organize their thoughts. Your students should take their time with this step, considering their subject carefully and thoroughly. Once they have gathered the obvious characteristics, they will need to try to describe their subject indirectly, in unusual ways. Perhaps they could describe it from a different person's point of view, from a new physical angle, or from a unique vantage point in time.

The web diagram shows "Tree" in the center, connected to circles labeled: roots (routes), branches, leaves (noun and verb), grows up, grows down, limbs, bark (noun and verb), trunk.

DRAFTING THE POEM

Building a Witty Puzzle

Next comes the especially fun part, in which your young writers play with their ideas. They will probably need to begin by writing a short prose description of their subject, relying on the characteristics they have written on their webs. They should then look for ways to turn that description into a riddle. How can plays on words or puns fit into the poem to give the readers hints? Can the spelling of a word be changed slightly, as Lewis did with "totally" and "because," to make the riddle more clever?

Although they don't have the read-aloud appeal of the more rhythmic and rhyming limerick (see page 32 for more on this), riddles too should be read aloud. It is important that your students share their poems with a writing partner during the composing process to give them a chance to listen for the sound of their words—always important in writing poetry. Reading the riddle aloud will also give the poet a sense of audience. It will let him or her know if the listener can follow the puzzle, if the listener thinks the poem is funny or clever, and if that listener can figure out the answer to the poem's riddle before getting frustrated.

EXTENDING THE LESSON

You could organize a riddle contest by posting the riddle poems outside your classroom or in the library and asking students to submit in writing the answers to the riddles. You could also have a Riddle Week and include a riddle as part of the morning announcements.

RESOURCES

While there are plenty of riddle books available, there aren't too many that are riddle poem books. J. Patrick Lewis has written two delightful books of riddle poems: *Riddle-icious* (Knopf, 1996) and *Riddle-lightful* (Knopf, 1998). *Riddle-Me-Rhymes* (Margaret McElderry, 1994), edited by Myra Cohn Livingston, is an anthology that includes riddle poems by the likes of Emily Dickinson and J.R.R. Tolkien, as well as by contemporary poets.

Chants and Street Rhymes

As I went up the apple tree,
All the apples fell on me.
Bake a pudding, bake a pie,
Did you ever tell a lie?
Yes, you did, you know you did,
You broke your mother's teapot lid.

Ooo-ah, wanna piece of pie,
Pie too sweet, wanna piece of meat,
Meat too tough, wanna ride a bus,
Bus was full, wanna ride a bull,
Bull too fat, want your money back,
Money too green, wanna jelly bean,
Jelly bean not cooked, wanna read a book,
Book not read, wanna go to bed.
So close your eyes and count to ten,
And if you miss, start all over again.

A, my name is Abby,
And my husband's name is Andy.
We come from Alaska,
And we sell aardvarks.
B, my name is Bonnie,
And my husband's name is Bert.
We come from Baltimore,
And we sell beads.

[…and so on through the alphabet]

Chants and Street Rhymes

Counting-Out Rhyme

(like "One Potato, Two Potato")

Bumblebee, bumblebee
Stung somebody on the knee
Stung a pig upon his snout
I say you are <u>out</u>!

Spelling Rhyme

New York
Knife and fork,
Bottle and cork,
That's the way
You spell New York.

Ball-Bouncing Rhyme

One, two, three, alary,
I spy old Miss Scary
Sitting on a dictionary
Just like a green canary.

Chants and Street Rhymes
Savoring the Street-Beat of Words

My first experience with a chant was on the baseball diamond across the street from my house when I was a kid. In a tight game, one of the players on our bench would begin the chant:

> Up the river, down the lake,
> The pitcher's got a bellyache.

Soon we were all chanting at the pitcher, hoping that our antics would disrupt his concentration. I'm sure it was that experience that led me to write a chant many years later that included these lines:

> Got the shivers, got the shakes,
> Pitcher's belly's full of snakes.

> Thunder book, lightning flash,
> Pitcher's got an itchy rash.

Can you recall some of the chants from your childhood? Perhaps you remember a jump-rope rhyme, or you remember that chant you recited as you walked to school:

> Step on a crack,
> And break your mother's back.

Or

> Step over a ditch,
> Your father's nose will itch.

A chant is a poem meant to be recited aloud. It nearly always has a line, phrase, or pattern repeated. Such repetition gives conviction and power to a chant just as it gives rhythm and music to a poem. So it has been since our ancestors sat around the campfire reciting chants to protect themselves from marauding beasts or to strengthen themselves for battle or for hunting.

EXPLORING THE POEM

Finding the Power in the Chant

Since rhythm and repetition are so important to the chant, that is a good place to start your lesson. Ask your students if they are familiar with any chants or jump-rope rhymes. As they recite their chants, record them on a cassette so you can replay them together to listen to the rhythm and repetition. Make sure your students can feel the beat. As they listen, have them clap their hands or gently slap their thighs to the rhythm.

Next, give the students the Poetry Pages, and have two small groups give choral readings of the chants as the rest of the class softly claps out the rhythm. This will help everyone get the feel of the kind of poetry they are about to write.

DRAFTING THE POEM

Rhythm From Memory, Words From the Heart

One way to get your students started on a chant is to ask them to write their own version of their favorite jump-rope or street rhyme. If they are not rope-jumpers, they might want to try writing a version of a rhyme from the Poetry Pages. One way to do this is to keep the rhythm of the chant in mind and fill in new words to the same beat, putting the repetitions and rhymes in the same spots as in the model chant. This step requires a lot of out-loud composing, so be prepared for a classroom full of constructive chatter.

EXTENDING THE LESSON

Since the chant must be read aloud for full effect, I suggest a program of oral presentations, complete with jump-rope demonstrations by those who have written jump-rope rhymes. Some chants work well with two students presenting the poems, one reading the body of the poem and another reading the repeating line. You might want to videotape or audiotape the presentation. Having a recording of the chants will prove helpful the next time you present this lesson, not to mention the fun you and your students will have reliving the program!

RESOURCES

Two great books of street rhymes are *Miss Mary Mack and Other Children's Street Rhymes* (Morrow, 1990) collected by Joanna Cole and Stephanie Almenson, and *Anna Banana: 101 Jump-Rope Rhymes* (Morrow, 1989) collected by Joanna Cole. For a more international flavor, you can try *Street Rhymes Around the World* (Boyds Mills, 1992) collected by Jane Yolen.

Two-Liners

Gums

My gums hold my teeth in place,
Which means a great deal to my face.

Blanket Hog

When my brother hogs the blanket
The only thing to do is yank it.

—both by PBJ

The Cow

The cow is of the bovine ilk;
One end is moo, the other, milk.

The Mule

In the world of mules
There are no rules.

The Fly

The Lord in His wisdom made the fly
And then forgot to tell us why.

—three by Ogden Nash

Two-Liners
Making Brevity the Soul of Wit

Writing these short poems may be as close as your students come to writing one-liners. A two-liner is a humorous poem that is made of two rhyming lines; it is a funny couplet. Like most good poems, a good two-liner will be the result of keen observation—of animals, everyday objects, or situations. A good two-liner, however, must put that observation into a humorous two-line poem that has both rhythm and rhyme.

EXPLORING THE POEM

Paring Observations to Their Core

When your students read the couplets on the Poetry Page, they will surely notice that the poems have end rhyme and a bouncy rhythm. Pressed to look more closely, they may notice that the poems are all observations. The poet offers these observations in a humorous fashion, of course. The most important thing about two-liners, however, is that they go beyond mere description to get at the essentials of the subject.

In "The Cow," for example, Nash writes with a steady rhythm and offers a clever rhyme. He also puts forward the bare bones about the cow—it moos and gives milk. The key to writing a good two-liner is to look for the essence of an object or a situation and to express that essence in a clever and original way.

BRAINSTORMING

Studying Creatures, Great and Small

To begin your lesson, you could tell your students that their first two-liner will be about animals. With the entire class working on one topic, you can bring in books and posters that will support the topic. You might, for instance, bring in a copy of *Ogden Nash's Zoo* and share some of his poems with your students. (Nearly all of the poems in the book are a bit longer than two lines, but they can give the students a chance to read what Nash noticed about these animals.) After you have shared some poems, you can give your students a chance to look through some picture books of animals. Students might also research an animal on the Internet or at the library.

When they have selected the animal they are going to write about, your students should take notes on that creature. They should jot down the obvious characteristics of the animal—size, shape, color, etc.—as well as their own reactions and feelings to the beast.

DRAFTING THE POEM

Finding the Beauty of the Beast

Drafting a two-liner is fun. Encourage your students to sit back, relax, and see where their drafting takes them. They need not worry about rhythm and rhyme at this point. The important thing is to get their words down on paper.

As the students work on their first drafts, ask them to:

- ◉ capture details, especially those that are unique or telling

- ◉ start with obvious observations, but focus on piercing ones

- ◉ find something humorous in the animal's appearance, behavior, or function

- ◉ collect puns and double-meaning words about the subject, like an elephant's "trunk" or a rhino's "horn"

- ◉ find a clever way to express the observations, perhaps by using unusual points of view or perspectives

Sometimes a first draft of a couplet will come out with a rhythm and rhyme already in it. If so, students can work on refining those elements as they revise. Other students will need to bring rhythm and rhyme into their words gradually as they tinker with and perfect their poems.

After your students have written an animal two-liner (or maybe a pair of them), and they have a feel for the technique, you might give them the chance to write about a subject of their own choosing, using the same process.

EXTENDING THE LESSON

If your students begin by writing animal two-liners, they could easily put together a book of poems like *Ogden Nash's Zoo*, complete with hand-drawn illustrations or photos from magazines or the Internet.

You can extend the lesson by giving your students a chance to write a quatrain (a stanza of four lines that most often rhyme). Your students might like the freedom that four lines gives them to express their observations in a clever, less brief manner. To start this follow-up lesson, give your students the Poetry Page on page 17. Read over the poems with your kids, and ask them to pick out some of the playful things that Nash does with language, like the use of "narra" (instead of "narrow") to rhyme with "Sahara," or the use of "golphin" (instead of "golfing") to rhyme with and resemble "dolphin." This can inspire them to create their own clever turns of phrase and spellings for their two-liners or quatrains.

RESOURCES

As described above, *Ogden Nash's Zoo* (Stewart, Tabori, & Chang 1987) has great animal poems to use as models for two-liners and quatrains or simply to enjoy.

Writing Funny Bone Poems Scholastic Professional Books

Quatrains

(TWO TWO-LINERS PUT TOGETHER)

by Ogden Nash

The Ostrich

The ostrich roams the great Sahara.
Its mouth is wide, its neck is narra.
It has such long and lofty legs,
I'm glad it sits to lay its eggs.

The Porpoise

I kind of like the playful porpoise,
A healthy mind in a healthy corpus.
He and his cousin, the playful dolphin,
Why they like swimmin like I like golphin.

The Termite

Some primal termite knocked on wood
And tasted it, and found it good,
And that is why your Cousin May
Fell through the parlor floor today.

Brat Poems

by X. J. Kennedy

In her upside-down umbrella
Going for a boat ride, Ella
Met while paddling through the sewer
A giant rat.

        One Ella fewer.

Told to wash Pooch, awful Arch
Dipped the dog in laundry starch,
Making Pooch's hair stand stiffer—
Ain't that cute?

        I beg to differ.

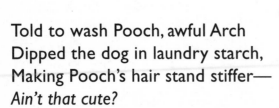

At the ostrich cage, Will Wick,
Warned that ostriches can kick,
Scoffed, "Oh yeah?" and turned his bottom—
That's precisely where it got him.

From the butcher shop Winona
Swiped a three-foot-long bologna,
Munched and munched and when all through,
Turned a lovely shade of blue.

Brat Poems
Dastardly Deeds and Just Deserts

Although his poems are prized for many, perhaps loftier, reasons, I know I can always turn to X. J. Kennedy's children's poems when I need a laugh. Among his works is *Brats*, a delightful collection of more than forty poems about kids who are…well, who are brats. He followed up his first collection with two other books of brat poems: *Fresh Brats* and *Drat These Brats!*

In a brat poem, tone is everything. Even though something unpleasant happens to each of the kids after their naughtiness—Ella gets devoured by a giant rat, Will Wick gets kicked in his bottom—we know that the poet writes of such consequences with a light heart and a tongue in his cheek. So, even though your students will be writing about annoying kids and dastardly deeds, help them to understand that a brat poem is fun, not mean.

Although each of the poems on the Poetry Page is four lines long (two couplets), the brat poems that Kennedy includes in his books are occasionally eight or ten lines long. Nonetheless, I'd suggest that you begin by having your students write four-line poems until they get into the swing of the brat poems. Of course, if they need more lines to tell a longer story, they should have the opportunity to do that.

EXPLORING THE POEM

CHARACTER

SETTING

WHAT CHARACTER DOES

WHAT HAPPENS TO CHARACTER

Mini-Stories of Crime and Punishment

Each brat poem is actually a very short story. After you or some students have read the poems on the Poetry Page aloud, ask the class to look for the story, and the story elements, in each poem. In almost every case, there is a character and a setting for the poem; in other words, a person and a time and/or a place where the action takes place. For example, Winona is in the butcher shop, and Will is at the ostrich cage. Because each poem is a story, there is a narrative thread to it; in other words, something happens. For example, Winona swipes a huge bologna, and Ella rides in an upside-down umbrella. Finally, each story comes to a satisfying conclusion, i.e., each brat must pay some price for his or her behavior—Winona gets sick, Ella gets eaten, and Will gets a kick in the bottom.

To help students visualize the components of each poem, you can give them a worksheet with spaces for character, setting, action, and consequences (see illustration). As they do the analyses of the poems necessary to fill in the spaces in this worksheet, they will become familiar with the elements they need to put into their own poems. You can give them another blank copy of the worksheet to help them organize their ideas as they brainstorm for their own brat poems.

BRAINSTORMING

Seeing Material in Mischief

One way to help your kids get ideas for their poems is to begin with a class brainstorming session to come up with a list of bratty things to do. I suspect they will have no trouble generating such devilish ideas. (Of course, you should feel free to add your own bratty ideas!) As the discussion gains steam, write all appropriate suggestions on the board. No doubt there will be an idea or two that isn't in the lighthearted spirit of the activity, but when these come up it will give you a chance to remind your students that the point of the activity is to write a good poem that is full of fun, not meanness.

Another way to get students to generate ideas is ask them to think about types of behavior that they don't like (for example, shoving in the hall or cutting into line). This annoying behavior could serve as the action in their poem. For example, they could write about someone who cuts into line and, as a consequence, must always go to the back of the longest line. You must be on guard, however, that this angle of brainstorming does not bring forth, in poetry, bloodthirsty calls for vengeance for some experience the writer has endured. Remind students to keep the tone of the poem light and amusing.

Your students might want to begin brainstorming ideas for their poem by coming up with an interesting name or one for which they find an amusing rhyme. Note how Kennedy finds amusing rhymes for his fun names: "Winona" and "bologna," "Arch" and "starch."

DRAFTING THE POEM

Telling the Tales

Many students feel more comfortable writing their first draft as a prose sentence or two, just to get their ideas down on the page. Once they have the general idea of the narrative part of their poem, they can begin to shape those ideas into two couplets. You might have rhyming dictionaries ready to aid your young writers.

As your students progress with their poems, you can circulate around the room and read over their shoulders. When you find a particularly good start, ask the student if you can read the poem aloud. As you read works in progress, talk about the sound of the poem, particularly the rhythm. The best way for students to hear the rhythm in Kennedy's poems, and in their own poems, is to read the poems out loud and listen. While the rhythm of these poems is not as important as it is in a limerick, for example, it is still distinctive, and your students should try to imitate it in their own poems.

EXTENDING THE LESSON

Your students could, of course, create their own book of brat poems. They could also illustrate their poems as comic strips, with each panel depicting a few lines of the poem. Since the brats in the poems do things considered ill-mannered, your class might also want to use the writings to create a sort of *Miss Manners's Guide to Bad Behavior.*

RESOURCES

If you'd like to read about more brats, look for Kennedy's three volumes of brat poems, all published by McElderry: *Brats* (1986), *Fresh Brats* (1990), and *Drat These Brats!* (1993).

Senryu

Brothers and sisters
blinded by love, no one sees
what the puppy left.

Sister read my book,
charming bookmark on page twelve...
saltine cracker crumbs.

First day, new school year,
backpack harbors a fossil ...
last June's cheese sandwich.

—three by Kristine O'Connell George

Solitary crow
calls cousin in distant pine
with its caw-ing card.

—by PBJ

Senryu
Finding Humor in Humanity

Your students may be familiar with the haiku, a short poetic form that originated in Japan about a century ago. Like the haiku, the senryu is made up of seventeen syllables written in three lines of five, seven, and five syllables. Strictly speaking, the difference between the two forms is that the senryu is written with wit and humor and is about human nature rather than about the natural world. As you can see, some of the senryu on the Poetry Page broaden the definition a bit since they are about the natural world. I allow students to write senryu about nature as long as their poems are witty and clever.

The senryu was originally only part of a long sequence of three-line poems—haiku and senryu—written by many different poets as part of a competition. The senryu parts tell of human events and actions while the haiku parts describe nature. This long poem composed of these parts is called a *regna*. Such poetry-writing competitions were quite popular in the 1700s, but it took many years for the senryu and the haiku to be liberated from the regna and recognized as poetic forms in themselves.

What is important about the haiku is important about the senryu: Poets should not be slaves to the syllable count. Yes, a senryu should try to emulate the classic form, but never at the expense of the content of the poem. In other words, as long as the poem follows the *spirit* of the poetic form, an occasional line can be a syllable too long or too short.

EXPLORING THE POEM

Chuckling and Counting

Distribute copies of the Poetry Page, and ask your students to read it, sharing their observations about the form and content of the poems. They may recognize the haiku form but be confused because these poems are not necessarily about nature. They will, I hope, see the humor.

After you discuss what the class has noticed, ask your students to read the poems again, this time marking off the syllables as they read. They will find that nearly all the poems are written in seventeen syllables with the traditional 5-7-5 division of those syllables.

BRAINSTORMING

Watching Humanity

Despite the differences between the haiku and senryu, they do have one very important thing in common: Both are the result of careful observation. So, you might begin your brainstorming session by asking students to name some good places to observe people and their human nature, such as the mall, the library, or the cafeteria.

The next step is to begin observing. Students are likely to be amused by what they find: a man who rides a bike while smoking a cigarette, or a girl who cries when she breaks up with her boyfriend, only to be seen holding hands with a different boy the very next day. It is, however, important to remind your students that the senryu is not meant to give them a chance to make fun of someone. Rather it is meant to point out those quirky things that we all have in common.

If you expand the definition of senryu, it gives kids the chance to write with wit and humor about the natural world as well as about human quirks. Then, students' observation posts will often be outdoors.

While some students might get an idea from observing, others might come up with a pun or a play on words and begin their poem from that point. For example, when I wrote the last senryu on the Poetry Page, I was watching crows calling to one another from the trees. I suddenly heard the similarity between *calling* and *cawing*. The rest of the poem grew from that play on words.

DRAFTING THE POEM

Adding Punch Lines to Insight

After your students have spent some time observing human nature or the natural world, or after they have spent some time playing with words and creating puns, they can begin drafting their senryu. Remind them that:

- ◉ the poem must be built of details from their observations

- ◉ it must *not* be a forum for them to complain or make fun of someone

- ◉ the third line of a senryu is something like the punch line of a good joke, and it may be where the play on words or the unexpected twist lies

EXTENDING THE LESSON

Since the senryu was originally part of a regna, you might want to give your young writers a chance to write such a long, collaborative poem. Each student could illustrate his or her senryu and they could be compiled into a booklet.

RESOURCES

The Haiku Handbook: How to Write, Share, and Teach Haiku (Kodansha International, 1985) by William J. Higginson, with Penny Harter, discusses senryu in detail and offers some fine examples.

Epitaphs

Here lies Johnny Yeast
Pardon me for not rising.

Here lies the body of Jonathan Blake
Stepped on the gas instead of the brake.

On the 22nd of June
Jonathan Fiddle
went out of tune.

Here lays Butch,
We planted him raw.
He was quick on the trigger
But slow on the draw.

Here lies the body of our Anna,
Done to death by a banana.
It wasn't the fruit that laid her low,
But the skin of the thing that made her go.

Epitaphs
Giggles From Six Feet Under

I was excited the very first time I prepared to have my students write epitaphs. My lesson plan was spectacular; I was sure they would respond with extraordinary poems! The lesson was a total flop. Oh, the students wrote lovely lines about dead people, but they weren't epitaphs, and they weren't funny. So I went back over my lesson, and I reread their poems in an attempt to find out what had gone wrong. Soon I realized that the fun was completely missing from their poems. The lines had none of the punning and playfulness that are common in many of the best epitaphs. I knew I had to find a way to put the fun back in these poems about the deceased.

Epitaphs are special poems about dead people. They are short poems—usually no longer than four lines—that are generally written in couplets or with alternate lines rhyming. Because epitaphs adorn tombstones, they are meant to be a lasting reminder of that person, often a tribute. Some epitaphs make an observation about a person's life or a person's character. Others make a comment about a person's profession or occupation. Some comment on the way in which the person died. All the good ones, however, have a clever twist or pun that brings a smile to our lips even as we remember the dearly departed. (Even when we never knew them.)

EXPLORING THE POEM

"Tom Swifties" and "How's Business?"

As I mentioned above, my first epitaph-writing unit flopped because I had not properly emphasized the importance of humor in the tombstone verse. How could I change that? I realized that one way to give the kids some practice in the fine art of punning was to let them play a couple of word games. The two worksheets at the end of the unit introduce students to two language games that might help them develop their pun-manship, "Tom Swifties" (see page 29) and "How's Business?" (see page 30). Before you introduce the idea of writing an epitaph, let your students try their hand at these games.

"Tom Swifties" pay homage to that pulp-fiction hero popular from the turn of the century until the start of World War II. They use a pun to describe how a person says something. For example, "'I really need a shower,' Tom said gamely," or, "'Stop hounding me,' Tom barked," or, "'There's too much vinegar in the dressing,' Tom said acidly." Lots of fun!

In "How's Business?" someone asks another person how his or her business is going, and that person replies with a outrageous pun. For example, if you ask a dentist, "How's business?" she might reply, "Boring." Or if you asked a dry cleaner, "How's business?" he might say, "Spotty." Or a veterinarian might say that her business is "Beastly."

BRAINSTORMING

Creating the Deceased

As you and your students read the epitaphs on the Poetry Page, ask them what they can figure out about the poems (i.e., how the subject dies, funny puns drawn on names, or what the names or puns say about the deceased's occupation). You can write their responses on the board where the list can grow visibly as the lesson progresses.

To help the class get started on their own poems, give your writers some time to think about some subjects for their epitaphs. On the board, you can write some areas to explore in their brainstorming: occupation, personal life, character, and manner of death. For example, ask your students which occupation might make a good subject for an epitaph. As students brainstorm, remind them to be thinking of puns that might go with their subject suggestions. For example, a sander's life might have been rough, or the elevator operator might have been last seen falling into the elevator shaft and saying something like, "Going down?" Some people are better punsters than others, so you might want to have your students brainstorm in small groups. Encourage your students to look back at their responses to the "Tom Swifties" and "How's Business?" to get ideas.

You can also brainstorm specific persons about whom students could write an epitaph. Perhaps they might write about a favorite musician or a popular politician, a soap-opera star or a talk-show host. There are a lot of possibilities, and such an epitaph might lead the students to think more carefully about some of the people held in high regard in our culture.

DRAFTING THE POEM

Making the Verse Fit for a Tomb

As in other instances, students may want to start by writing their ideas in prose form. By doing this, they can begin weaving together the person, profession, manner of death, and any other parts of the poem they have thought up without worrying yet about creating the epitaph structure. By this time, the wordplay and puns are already a part of the description of the deceased's life, and students need only play with their writing to bring out the funniest arrangement of words and phrases. Next, of course, comes the tweaking of the poem into the proper form, with rhythm, rhymes, and a touch of (usually) sarcastic reverence.

EXTENDING THE LESSON

Since epitaphs are poems that appear on tombstones, students could make posters shaped like tombstones on which they can write their poems. They might also look for a picture in a magazine or a newspaper of someone who looks just like the subject of their poem to add to their grave sites.

Because epitaphs are about people, this is a good assignment to use in other curriculum areas. Your class could, for example, write an epitaph about a scientist or a musician or a personality from history. Students could also write an epitaph for a character from a book or a play.

RESOURCES

If you are looking for more epitaphs, there's no better place to start searching than on the Internet. You can start with **www.underworld-tales.com/epitaphs.html,** but nearly any search engine will give you plenty of Web sites to choose from if you search with the key word "epitaph." When sifting through the results, you will find that sites that mention "poetry" in their description will often be closer to what you need than the others.

Tom Swifties

1. "That's the last time I'll pet a lion," Tom said _____.

2. "I forgot what to buy," Tom said _____.

3. "I've struck oil!" Tom said _____.

4. "Buy me something to drink," Tom said _____.

5. "I love fairy tales," Tom said _____.

6. "Get away from the dynamite," Tom said _____.

7. "I keep banging my head on things," Tom said _____.

8. "I don't like hot dogs," Tom said _____.

9. "I need a pencil sharpener," Tom said _____.

10. "I'll try to dig it up for you," Tom said _____.

11. "Mush!" Tom said _____.

12. "My pencil is dull," Tom said _____.

13. "Let's go see the movie *Aladdin,*" Tom said _____.

14. "I have to renew my subscriptions," Tom said _____.

15. "I don't think I'll be in school tomorrow," Tom said _____.

frankly	gravely	absently
dryly	offhandedly	crudely
huskily	explosively	bashfully
listlessly	grimly	periodically
disappointedly	genially	bluntly

How's Business?

1. "How's business, trash collector?"

2. "How's business, carpet salesperson?"

3. "How's business, astronomer?"

4. "How's business, prizefighter?"

5. "How's business, weight watcher?"

6. "How's business, florist?"

7. "How's business, taxi driver?"

8. "How's business, exterminator?"

9. "How's business, candle maker?"

10. "How's business, knife maker?"

11. "How's business, pillow maker?"

12. "How's business, drill operator?"

13. "How's business, refrigerator salesperson?"

14. "How's business, housewrecker?"

15. "How's business, traffic cop?"

lousy	slow	looking up
dull	wicked	fair (fare)
down	boring	smashing
picking up	blooming	rugged
sluggish	gaining	not so hot

Writing Funny Bone Poems Scholastic Professional Books

Limericks
by April Halprin Wayland

There once was a cat who loved rice
While soy sauce was her favorite spice
With chopsticks she ate
Vegetarian plates
Then bowed to applause from the mice.

There once was a ghost dude named Dave
Who lived at the beach in a cave
On Manhattan Beach turf
He invisibly surfed
Scaring up some gigantic rad waves.

The Peanut Guy he had a dream
Whenever he threw, fans would scream
With each bag he sold
A great throw he'd unfold
They watched him, ignoring their team.

A frog who weighed nearly a ton
Came courting Amelia DeGrunn
When he hopped up to kiss her
He found that he'd missed her
She'd suddenly gone for a run.

Limericks
Good Clean Fun

When your students hear a limerick read aloud, there will be instant recognition on most of their faces. The limerick is one of the most widely recognized poetic forms, especially with kids. It sounds so light and bouncy that the listener is ready to smile. However, writing a good limerick takes a good ear as well as a good sense of humor.

The limerick is a five-line poem, in which lines three and four are shorter by a beat than the other three lines. Specifically, lines one, two, and five have three stressed (or accented) syllables, while lines three and four have only two stressed syllables. The metrical feet used in a limerick are called iambic, like the words *until* and *because*, and anapestic, like the words *disagree* and *understand*. The rhyme scheme for a limerick is *aabba*, which means that lines one, two, and five have the same end rhyme, represented by *a*. Lines three and four also have the same end rhyme, represented by *b*. Most young students construct the beat and rhyme of their poem by imitating other limericks rather than by following a series of rules, and this is to be expected and applauded.

EXPLORING THE POEM

Hearing the Rhyme, Feeling the Beat

Since the limerick relies so heavily on rhythm and rhyme, it's important that your students hear the rhythm and rhyme and see how both are crucial to a good limerick. Give each student a copy of the Poetry Page, and ask a few students to read the poems aloud. Ask your students what they hear in the poems. They will hear the rhyme, which is obvious, but they might need some help in discerning and discussing "the beat" of the poem.

If your students are old enough, you can talk about stressed syllables and explain the difference between iambic and anapestic feet by writing examples on the board. Ask students to supply other words with the same stressed syllables.

Once the students have come up with suitable examples of the different kinds of metrical feet, ask them to read through the limericks again, this time marking the stressed and unstressed syllables. They will no doubt notice that not all the words are two- and three-syllable words. Often, however, shorter words combine with other words to create the appropriate rhythm for a limerick. Remind the students that not every metrical poem is perfectly metrical, with exactly the correct number of stressed and unstressed syllables in each line.

Of course, some students are too young to understand and enjoy finding patterns of stressed syllables—for them, hearing the separate syllables is work enough. In this case, students should skip this step and rely on their keen ears to help them choose the right words for their limericks.

BRAINSTORMING AND DRAFTING THE POEM

The First Line Is the First Step

Before your students begin drafting their poem, ask them to read through the limericks again and see if they notice anything else about the way they are written. They may notice that limericks generally start with one of these two types of lines: "There once was a boy/girl named _____," or "There once was a boy/girl from _____." Although your students should feel free to begin their limerick in any way that works, they could begin the draft of their first limerick using one of these two lines. When they have written their first line, they might brainstorm a list of words that rhyme with the last word of their first line. If they haven't already used one, your kids would probably appreciate an introduction to rhyming dictionaries at this point.

A word of caution: The last line of a limerick is usually the most difficult to write. It must fit the rhythm and rhyme of a limerick, but it also must make sense in the poem. Many students write a fifth line that has the correct rhyme and the rhythm but doesn't make contextual sense. If your young writers think of the limerick as a *very* short story in which something happens to a character, that might help them to write satisfying conclusions to their poems.

EXTENDING THE LESSON

After your students have written a limerick or two with a standard opening line, encourage them to try a different opening line, like Wayland did in the second and third poems on the Poetry Page. Students can get more ideas by reading some of Edward Lear's limericks. (After all, many people credit him with "inventing" the form.) To complete your lesson on limericks, you might give your students the opportunity to illustrate one of their poems on a poster, which would look great hanging from the walls of your classroom or in the corridor near your room.

RESOURCES

Edward Lear's Nonsense Omnibus (Penguin, 1986) is a must for your classroom library. It contains all the original pictures, verses, and stories from his major books. *Uncle Switch* (McElderry, 1997) by X. J. Kennedy is a collection of "loony limericks," with zany color illustrations. It is a good example for students who would like to make a book of their limericks.

"I Spy" Poems

by Jean Marzollo

I spy a magnet, a monkey, a mouse
A squash, two flags, five 4's, a house;
A bird on a B, an exit sign,
A UFO, and a valentine.

I spy a rabbit, a rhyming snake.
An apple, a shark, and a birthday cake;
An unfinished word, a whale, two dimes,
Tic-tac-toe, and JUAN three times.

I spy an acorn, a cricket, a 3,
A shell in a nest, a shell from the sea;
Three feathers, two frogs, a ladybug, too,
Ten drops of water, and thread that is blue.

I spy a frog, a checkerboard 3,
A zigzag 4, and a zebra Z;
A rabbit, an arrow, a girl named DOT,
Six red blocks, and the missing knot.

—from I Spy School Days: A Book of Picture Riddles

"I Spy" Poems
Keen Eyes and Good Couplets

When my daughter was younger, she missed me when I left to visit schools in other states, so before I went away, I would hide clues around the house for her. If she solved the puzzle of the clue—and she never missed one—it would lead her to a small treat. Occasionally, I would write my clues in verse, imitating the wonderful *I Spy* books filled with Walter Wick's amazing color photographs and what author Jean Marzollo calls "verse riddles." The object of these books is to read the verses and find the things they refer to in the two-page photographs. The verses are not technically riddles because the reader is looking for items in a picture rather than trying to figure out what is described in the verse, but they can still be lots of fun in your classroom.

EXPLORING THE POEM

Scrutinizing Verse and Photographs

Begin your lesson on the "I Spy" poem by getting a few copies of some of the *I Spy* books. The Poetry Page by itself won't do the trick since it doesn't have the photographs of the objects to go with it. Your school library and the local library should have copies of many books in the series. Try to get enough books so you can give one book to each group of five or six students. Let each group explore the pictures and the verses. Let them see that sometimes the things in plain sight are the most difficult to see. Once they have had a chance to solve some riddles in the book, tell your students that they are ready to get started writing an "I Spy" poem about things in the classroom.

BRAINSTORMING

Detecting and Recording

Whether students work alone or in small groups, the first step is the same: They will need to investigate the classroom looking for objects that could be included in the poem. Objects need to be visible, large or small, but that doesn't mean that they have to be obvious. Using the *I Spy* book as a model, remind the students that sometimes only part of an object is visible. Kids can record a list of objects in the classroom that would make good subjects for "I Spy" verses and a brief description of where the objects are located—in case they forget.

DRAFTING THE POEM

Creating the Clues

Once students have compiled a hefty list of likely objects, they can start fashioning their couplets. Remind them that writing an "I Spy" poem is like writing a riddle in that the puzzle should be challenging without being impossible. Your writers should explore ways to be clever in their poems. For example, one verse in *I Spy: School Days Riddles* tells readers to find "the missing knot." The photograph on the left-hand page includes a puzzle showing a rope with one small puzzle piece missing. That puzzle piece, which pictures the rope's knot, is on the facing page! Another verse tells readers to seek "a grandfather clock." Most people look for a large clock, when, in fact, the clock in question is a picture on the cover of a book, partially obscured by a notebook, at that! Perhaps your students will use puns and words with double meanings, as they have in writing other poems. In one of the *I Spy* books, for example, the reader is asked to look for a trunk, which turns out to be the trunk of an elephant!

Your young writers need to be aware of two elements in this form of poetry. First, of course, is the rhyme. The poem must be written in couplets. Beyond that, remind your students that their verses must sound smooth. Each line in the *I Spy* books contains about ten syllables, and the stressed syllables fall in similar places in each line. Make sure that your kids take the time to read their verses aloud so they can hear if they have captured the same rhythm as the original verses.

EXTENDING THE LESSON

Writing an "I Spy" poem about the classroom is good training for other similar poems your students can write. They can construct collages from magazine photographs and ads, and write their poems about their collages. A sheet of standard poster board is a size that allows space for lots of objects and, therefore, provides enough material for verses.

Try to share the best poems with other students. You could, for example, invite another class into your room to see if they can solve the classroom "I Spy" poems that your kids have written. Or you could organize a traveling "I Spy" show with your students, bringing their collages and poems to the classes of younger students to see if they can solve the verse. Many younger students will be quite familiar with the *I Spy* series, so explanations of the game are easy.

RESOURCES

There are many *I Spy* books, all published by Scholastic. Among the titles are *I Spy: Extreme Challenger* (2000), *I Spy: Fantasy* (1994), *I Spy: Gold Challenger* (1998), and *I Spy: Mystery* (1993). They're not just for kids!

"Can You Imagine?" Poems

by Paul B. Janeczko

Can You Imagine?

Trees without bark
Noah without his ark

Cows without moos
Hyenas with the blues

Limbs without bones
Wrestling without groans

Bananas without peels
A car without wheels

Shoes without soles
Buttons without holes

Books without pages
A zoo without cages

Sheep without fleece
A world at peace.

"Can You Imagine?" Poems
Composing New Worlds Through Rhyme

Writing "Can You Imagine?" poems is a fun activity for several reasons. First, it gives students an opportunity to let their imaginations kick into high gear. By looking at commonplace objects and imagining how things might be different, young poets can write about a pretend world, often with humorous results. My poem, for example, asks the reader to imagine things like "Bananas without peels" and "Books without pages." (The latter doesn't seem so far-fetched these days with e-books!) Further, writing this kind of poem is perfect as a collaborative-learning activity. Kids can work in pairs to create a long poem, or each member of the class can write a couplet (two rhyming lines of poetry) that can be part of a class poem.

EXPLORING THE POEM

Discovering Patterns

Give your students a copy of "Can You Imagine?" from this section's Poetry Page, and ask someone to read the poem aloud. After the reading, ask your students what they noticed about the poem. Most will quickly note the word pattern and the pairs of rhyming lines. Others may notice the lines are short with a similar rhythm. Still others will notice that each line is about something common. These are all good observations, and they will help your students when they begin to write their own poems.

BRAINSTORMING

Noting Parts and Pieces

The way to begin writing this kind of poem is to choose a bunch of common things and then a few expected qualities or parts for each. If students get stuck, have them observe the things around them to give them ideas. As they make lists, they should write down two or three qualities or parts of each object, not just one, since that opens more possibilities for finding the second, rhyming line. For example, for the common item "shoe" I wrote "Shoes without soles." I could also have written "Shoes without tongues." Then, of course, I would have written a different second line in that couplet—something like "Ladders without rungs."

Once your students have made lists, things get even more fun because the poetry writing can begin. In fact, students may not even wait until they have completed these lists. As soon as they write down a subject and some of its qualities, they may write a line for their poem. So be it. Let the poets write!

DRAFTING THE POEM

Composing Delightful Couplets

I suggest that you begin the drafting process by creating a few couplets orally with your class. Ask a student to suggest an opening line. For example, one might choose "A tree without roots." Now the class needs to find a rhyming line to complete the couplet. Someone might suggest "A firefighter without boots." Another student might offer "An owl without hoots" or "A soldier without salutes." You may want to point out the lines in the poem from the Poetry Page that don't contain the word "without." See if students can come up with a second line to their own couplet that doesn't contain that word. When your students have composed a few possibilities for second lines, you can decide as a class which ones make the best verses. Ask yourselves which ones make interesting or funny visual images. Which ones sound the most pleasing to the ear? Which ones have the strongest effects? After students have decided what makes a good couplet for this kind of poem, they are ready to begin work on their own.

Your students may rely on their lists. But they need not, of course, be limited by these lists. Often, when writing one thing, new things come to mind, and students should feel free to allow their thinking to go beyond their original ideas.

EXTENDING THE LESSON

A good "Can You Imagine?" poem will have some very amusing visual images. Ask your students to choose one couplet they have written that contains two images they could draw. These illustrated couplets can be put together into a class book. Such a book would be a wonderful addition to the class library. If you photocopy the book, you can make sure that the school library and all of your students have a copy. Of course, individual students who have written poems with many visual images might be interested in creating a book of their own.

RESOURCES

Your students could look through the books of their favorite funny poets, perhaps Shel Silverstein and Jack Prelutsky, searching for nonsense poems that follow a pattern that they could imitate. They could start with *Where the Sidewalk Ends* or *A Light in the Attic* (HarperCollins, 1974, 1981) by Silverstein, or *It's Raining Pigs and Noodles* (Greenwillow, 2000) by Prelutsky.

"I'd Rather Be..." Poems

by Paul B. Janeczko

I'd Rather Be

I'd rather be hands than feet
I'd rather be honest than cheat
I'd rather be cold than heat
I'd rather be Paul than Pete
I'd rather be a bed than a seat
I'd rather be a blanket than a sheet
I'd rather be corn than wheat
I'd rather be a woof than a tweet
I'd rather be a trick than a treat
I'd rather be sloppy than neat
I'd rather be sunshine than sleet
I'd rather be wood than concrete
I'd rather be huge than petite
I'd rather be sad than upbeat
I'd rather be new than repeat
I'd rather be tart than sweet
I'd rather be a road than a street
I'd rather be a part than complete
I'd rather be veggies than meat
I'd rather be a carrot than a beet

"I'd Rather Be..." Poems
Playful Wishes in Verse

I learned this activity from Sandra Brownjohn's book *To Rhyme or Not to Rhyme?* It's a great way for your students to work with rhyme in an entertaining way, whether they work as a class or as individuals.

The idea is simple. As the example on the Poetry Page shows, each line in the poem follows the pattern "I'd rather be _____ than _____," and all the end words rhyme. The important thing about this poem is that though it has the feel of nonsense, the two elements in each line do make sense together; the second part of each line must logically or linguistically follow the first part of the line. The fun of this poem comes from seeing how far you can push the rhyme—how many rhyming lines you can compose while still making sense.

EXPLORING THE POEM

Would You Rather Be Paul or Pete?

After your students have read the Poetry Page, ask them to identify the pattern in the poem. Your class will easily see the contrast in each line: "I'd rather be _____ than _____." They will also, of course, point out the end rhyme. It takes some keen study, however, to figure out the kinds of relationships between objects that make the poem work. Students tend to notice the opposites first, but there are other relationships present as well. Sometimes it is merely a matter of making a choice between two side-by-side, similar things, for example, "I'd rather be a road than a street." Students can think about why the poet would rather be one thing than the other, which might help them construct rhymes with meaning—not just marvelous sounds—when they make the poems on their own.

BRAINSTORMING

Rhymes Galore

Give students a copy of the worksheet on page 43, which contains the framework of this poem. At the top of the page is a space to write the sound of the rhyme they will be working with in the poem. For starters, I suggest that you supply the sound.

You could use some of these:

-un as in pun	-one as in cone	-ine as in dine
-out as in pout	-o as in know	-ight as in light

If you'd like more rhyming sounds to choose from, thumb through *The Scholastic Rhyming Dictionary* in which the sounds are organized alphabetically.

For this brainstorming session you can have the kids work in groups, since they can produce more rhymes that way. When the groups have had some time to work on their poems, ask them to read them aloud to the rest of the class.

DRAFTING THE POEM

A Variety of Schemes

I suggest that for their first individual poem, writers come up with rhymes on their own and don't use a rhyming dictionary. I like to let writers use the rhyming dictionary eventually, however, because it often introduces them to new words or reminds them of words they had forgotten. Even when your students have a list of rhyming words provided by the dictionary, they still need to do the thinking necessary to use those words properly in their poem.

There are many variations of "I'd Rather Be . . ." poems that poets might explore to make this activity more challenging. You could ask students to write this kind of poem in a different rhyme scheme. For example, instead of using the same end rhyme in all the lines, the poem could be composed of couplets. You might ask your students to write the rhyming lines in tercets (a stanza of three lines) or quatrains (a stanza of four lines). They could even rhyme every other line.

EXTENDING THE LESSON

If the class works on this activity together instead of individually, you could all have a lot of fun creating a "game show." To play, you begin by announcing an opening line. Each group then works in a corner of the room trying to write the longest rhyming poem that begins with that line. When the allotted time expires (five or ten minutes), each group reads its poem to the class. You and the class decide which lines are acceptable and can earn the team a point. After several rounds of poem writing, the team with the most points is declared the champion!

There is also a spontaneous oral version of the game. Students divide into small groups, and two teams compete at a time. Begin the game by presenting an opening line to one of the teams. That team must respond with an acceptable rhyming line within a time limit (I suggest you keep it short!). Then it is the other team's turn to add a line. This continues until one team cannot respond within the given time.

RESOURCES

To Rhyme or Not to Rhyme? (Hodder & Stoughton, 1994) by Sandra Brownjohn is packed with poetry-writing activities. Although the book is British and somewhat hard to find, it is worth the search.

Name _____ Date _____

WORKSHEET FOR
"I'd Rather Be..." Poems

Sound _____

I'd rather be _____ than _____.

I'd rather be _____ than _____.

I'd rather be _____ than _____.

I'd rather be _____ than _____.

I'd rather be _____ than _____.

I'd rather be _____ than _____.

I'd rather be _____ than _____.

I'd rather be _____ than _____.

I'd rather be _____ than _____.

I'd rather be _____ than _____.

I'd rather be _____ than _____.

I'd rather be _____ than _____.

I'd rather be _____ than _____.

I'd rather be _____ than _____.

Parodies

by Paul B. Janeczko

Old Mother Hubbard
Went to the cupboard
To fetch her laptop computer
But when she got there
The cupboard was bare
She had traded it in for a scooter

Jack, be nimble
Jack, be slick
Jack knew what investments to pick.

Tom, Tom the butcher's son
Ate a hot dog in a bun
The beef was bad
He cried, "Egad,"
Now no more food he takes from Dad.

Jack Sprat would watch TV
His wife would throw a fit
And so, one day she pulled the plug
And Jack was so mad he split.

Georgie Porgie, all a-flutter
Spied the jar of peanut butter
Spread some on a slice of bread
Ate it quick and then he fled.

Writing Funny Bone Poems Scholastic Professional Books

Parodies

A Twist of Wit in Old Favorites

A parody is writing that imitates other writing in a way that makes fun of the original, usually serious, work. A parody might also be written to mock the author of the original piece of writing. On the other hand, some parodies are just downright funny with no ulterior motives. While a parody might be funny in its own right, for it to really work, the reader must be familiar with the original piece. The humor must come in the contrast between the parody and the original.

EXPLORING THE POEM

Why Nursery Rhymes Work So Well

One of the easiest ways to get young writers to write parody poems is to ask them to imitate poems and nursery rhymes they already know. Parodies are particularly funny when students update a poem or write a piece that imitates yet contradicts the original. Nursery rhymes provide great material because they have a simple structure and are therefore easy to imitate. Many of them also have a subject that is easy to change drastically, by making it contemporary, for instance.

BRAINSTORMING

Nursery Rhymes for Fun and Fodder

You can begin your lesson by asking your students to read or recite any nursery rhymes they can remember. It is important to let your students hear many nursery rhymes aloud because the sound and rhythm of the poems will be important in their parody. You can supplement the poems they remember with the poems on the Poetry Page at the end of the unit. If you plan to work on parodies for several days, encourage the kids to bring in any nursery rhyme books they have at home. You can check the library for similar books to bring into the class to share with your students. Give your students some time to browse through the nursery rhymes, reminding themselves of their favorites. Somewhere in these stacks of nursery rhymes, students will eventually find a poem ripe for parody.

When your students have had sufficient time to read lots of nursery rhymes and have their rhythms running through their heads, you can give them the Poetry Page. Ask them to read silently . . . except for chuckles. Afterward, a couple of students can read the poems aloud. Ask the students what they notice about the poems. They should be able to articulate which elements of the originals are imitated in the parody. After this exercise their reading of the nursery rhymes will take on an entirely different meaning. Now students will be reading to see how they can have a little fun changing what they read!

DRAFTING THE POEM

Poking Fun at Mother Goose

Your students should be ready to begin drafting their poem once they have had time to read some nursery rhymes and some parodies of those poems. They could start by choosing a character from a rhyme and thinking about what new changes they can introduce to that character. For example, I made my Jack an investment banker rather than merely a kid who jumps over a candlestick. So they might take Humpty Dumpty or Little Bo Peep and update them. Humpty might be a jogger worried about his weight. Bo might ditch her sheep and become a vegetarian.

As your students work on their drafts, tell them that although they have license with the subject matter of a poem, they should try to remain faithful to the rhythm and rhyme scheme of the original. This is a good time to remind them that part of the writing process should be reading the poem aloud to listen to the music of the piece. Ask them to read their poem to a writing partner when they feel it is ready to be read aloud. Both reader and listener should be able to hear the beat of the original in the parody.

EXTENDING THE LESSON

As with most poetry, parodies are great for reading aloud, so your students could organize a performance for the class or for a large group of kindergarten kids or first graders. Or you could divide your class into small groups and have them visit the classrooms of younger kids and share parodies in their classrooms.

Because parodies of nursery rhymes are so much fun to read aloud, your students might be interested in producing a radio program of their poems, complete with music and sound effects. Perhaps one of your radio programs could even be broadcast over your school's morning announcements.

RESOURCES

One of my favorite book of parodies is *Roald Dahl's Revolting Rhymes* (Knopf, 1982), with illustrations by Quentin Blake. Dahl retells, in verse, six fairy tales including *Cinderella* and *Little Red Riding Hood*. It's hilarious stuff.

Mother Goose Rhymes

Jack and Jill
Went up the hill
To fetch a pail of water.
Jack fell down
And broke his crown,
And Jill came tumbling after.

Jack Sprat could eat no fat,
His wife could eat no lean;
And so, between them both, you see,
They licked the platter clean.

Humpty Dumpty sat on a wall,
Humpty Dumpty had a great fall.
All the King's horses and all the King's men
Couldn't put Humpty together again.

Old Mother Hubbard
Went to the cupboard,
To fetch her poor dog a bone;
But when she got there
The cupboard was bare,
And so the poor dog had none.

Little Jack Horner
Sat in the corner,
Eating his Christmas pie.
He put in his thumb,
And pulled out a plum,
And said, "What a good boy am I!"

Recommended Books About Teaching Poetry Writing

Dunning, Stephen, and William Stafford. *Getting the Knack: 20 Poetry Writing Exercises*. NCTE, 1992.

Fletcher, Ralph. *Breathing In, Breathing Out*. Heinemann, 1996.

_____. *What a Writer Needs*. Heinemann, 1992.

Glover, Mary Kenner. *A Garden of Poets*. NCTE, 1999.

Graves, Donald H. *Explore Poetry*. Heinemann, 1992.

Green, Benjamin. *Beyond Roses are Red, Violets are Blue*. Cottonwood Press, 1996.

Heard, Georgia. *For the Good of the Earth and the Sun*. Heinemann, 1989.

_____. *Awakening the Heart: Exploring Poetry in Elementary and Middle Schools*. Heinemann, 1998.

Janeczko, Paul B. *Favorite Poetry Lessons*. Scholastic, 1998.

_____. *Teaching 10 Fabulous Forms of Poetry*. Scholastic, 2000.

_____. *How to Write Poetry*. Scholastic, 1999.

_____. *Poetry From A to Z: A Guide for Young Writers*. Simon & Schuster, 1996.

Johnson, David M. *Word Weaving*. NCTE, 1990.

Kennedy, X. J., and Dorothy M. Kennedy. *Knock at a Star* (revised edition). Little, Brown, 1999.

King, Laurie, and Dennis Stoval. *Classroom Publishing*. Blue Heron Publishing, 1992.

Koch, Kenneth. *Making Your Own Days: the Pleasure of Reading and Writing Poetry*. Simon & Schuster, 1998.

Kohl, Herbert. *A Grain of Poetry*. HarperCollins, 1999.

Livingston, Myra Cohn. *Poem-Making: Ways to Begin Writing Poetry*. HarperCollins, 1991.

Lyon, George Ella. *Where I'm From: Where Poems Come From*. Absey & Co., 1999.

McClure, Amy A. *Sunrises and Songs: Reading and Writing Poetry in an Elementary Classroom*. Heinemann, 1990.

McVeigh-Schultz, Jane, and Mary Lynn Ellis. *With a Poet's Eye*. Heinemann, 1997.

Padgett, Ron, ed. *Handbook of Poetic Forms*. Teachers and Writers Collaborative, 1987.

Routman, Regie. *Kids' Poems: Teaching Third & Fourth Graders to Love Writing Poetry*. Scholastic, 2000.

Tucker, Shelley. *Painting the Sky*. Good Year Books, 1994.

_____. *Word Weavings*. Good Year Books, 1997.

Wilson, Lorraine. *Write Me a Poem*. Heinemann, 1994.

Wooldridge, Susan G. *Poemcrazy*. Clarkson Potter, 1996.